W9-DAX-745

Rabbits

Gerald and Julie Hawksley

Consultant: Dr. Stanley J. Truffini, DVM

CHILDRENS PRESS CHOICE
A Joshua Morris title selected for educational distribution

Illustrations by Gerald Hawksley.

Printed in Hong Kong

Contents

All About Rabbits

Pet rabbits are related to the type of rabbits that live wild in the countryside. They have many of the same features.

All rabbits have very long ears which can pick up the faintest sounds. They have large, stron hind legs and feet.

Rabbits are herbivores, which means that they feed on plant and never eat meat. They have long front teeth especially sha to tear grass and gnaw at woo

Wild rabbits live in groups. They use their feet to dig the holes and tunnels they live in, which are called burrows.

Although pet rabbits have homes provided for them, they still love to tunnel and dig.

Wild rabbits come out to feed at dawn and dusk. They graze on grass in the same way that cattle and sheep do.

Pet Rabbits

There are many types, or breeds, of rabbit, but most pets are either Dutch rabbits, English rabbits, or a mixture of both.

The Dutch rabbit can be black, brown or gray. It always has large patches of white on its body.

The English rabbit is white all over with bl
or brown markings.

hese more unusual breeds can also be kept as pets, but they 'ten need special care.

The Angora rabbit has very long fluffy fur, which needs regular brushing. Its hair can be collected and spun into wool to make soft warm sweaters.

The lop-eared rabbit has long ears which hang down to the ground. Its bedding must always be kept clean so that its ears do not get dirty.

The dwarf rabbit is the smallest breed of all. It has short ears and grows to about the size of a guinea pig.

Your New Rabbit

Rabbits are usually sold when they are three to six months old. Your pet shop will probably have lots for you to choose from. If you want an unusual breed try going to a rabbit show, where you can often bu a pet.

Choose an animal that looks lively and healthy, with bright eyes and a sleek coat. Its nose should be twitching and its ears should move in the direction of small sounds.

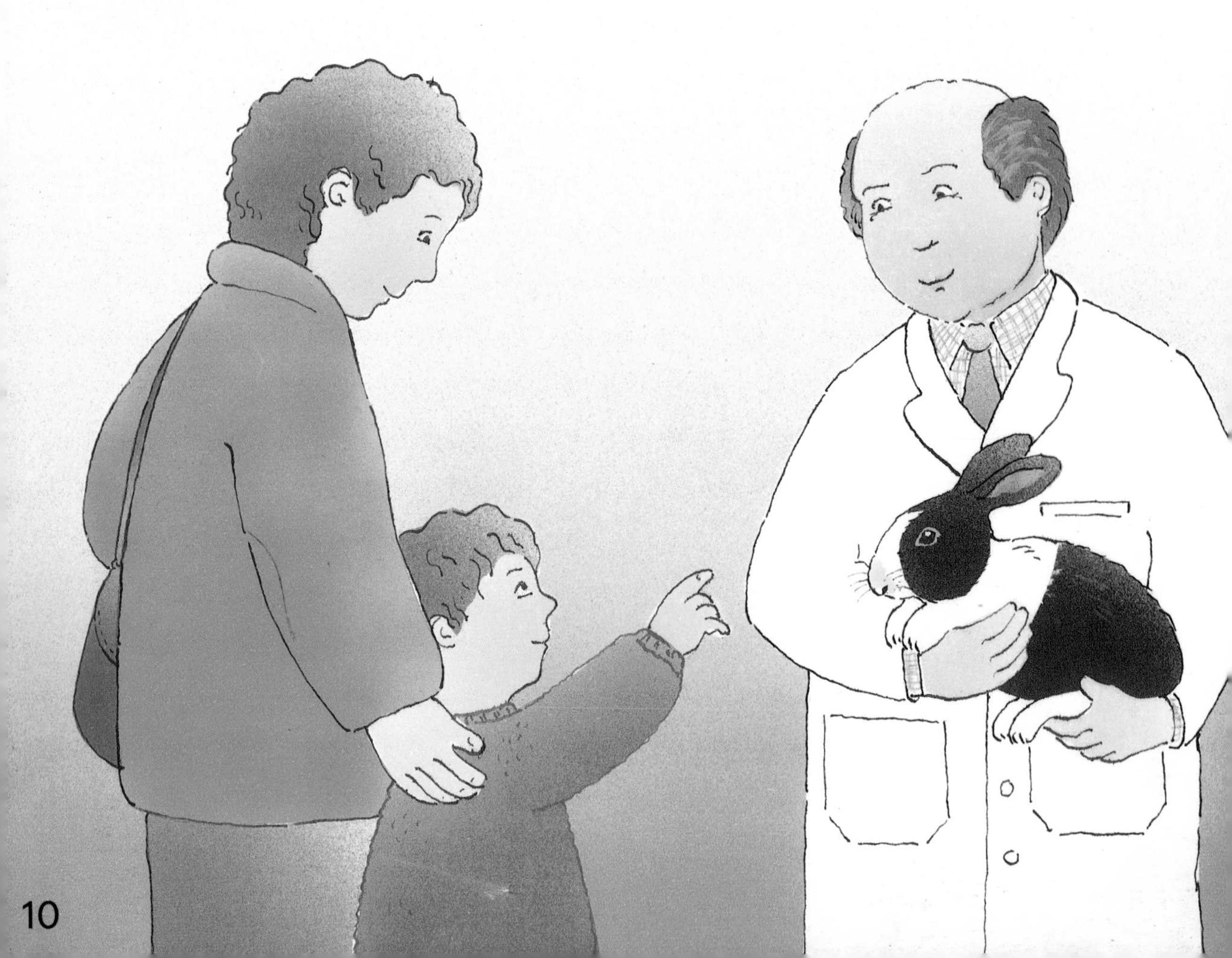

Remember to take along a strong box to carry your rabbit home in. Line it with newspaper or straw and make sure that it has plenty of small holes to let air in and will close tightly.

You could buy a box from the pet shop with air holes and strong carrying handles.

ve a hutch ready before you
.e your rabbit home so that it
; somewhere where it can get
ɜd to its new surroundings in
ɔce. Let your pet settle into its
w home for a while before you
k it up.

Your Rabbit's Home

The hutch will be your rabbit's home for a long time, so find the largest one you can. If it is outside it must keep out cold and damp. To stop cold drafts raise the hutch two to three feet off the ground by resting it on some wood or bricks.

If you like the idea of your rabbit having a companion, make sure that they are both females, and that the hutch is large enough for both of them to live together happily.

The hutch should be placed beside a wall or hedge, where it will be sheltered from the wind and the sun. You could get a roll-down cover for extra winter warmth.

Make sure your rabbit has a cozy, quiet sleeping box behin a wooden screen in the hutch. Cover this part of the floor wit plenty of straw or hay to keep your pet snug and warm.

The hutch roof should slope backwards so that rain will easily drain off it.
Outside the sleeping box there should be a roomy living area. Cover this floor with clean sawdust or shavings.
ut wire netting on the front of ne hutch, so your rabbit can e out, and so you will be ole to watch it eating and oving around. Make sure the utch doors are strong, with ood hinges and latches.

Mealtime

Rabbits eat hay and special dried food which pet shops sell. They also like vegetable scraps, which should be rinsed in water before you feed them to your rabbit. You could also give them a few dandelion leaves from your yard.

Ceramic bowls are best for food because they won't tip over very easily. Throw away old food and clean the bowls regularly.

As a treat give your rabbit tidbits such as carrots, nuts, toasted bread and sunflower seeds for a shiny coat.

Most rabbits enjoy eating fruit. You could try putting out small pieces of apple, pear or melon.

See that there is always fresh water in the hutch. You could buy a special drinking bottle to hang up. This will help to keep the water fresh and pleasant to drink.

Your pet will like to be fed at the same time each day. But do not put out too much food at once, because rabbits can quickly get fat. Two small meals a day should be plenty.

Your Rabbit's Health

Your rabbit will need exercise to help it stay fit, so ask a grown-up to make a special exercise run for it in the yard. This is a frame covered with netting — it will keep your rabbit safe from other animals but give it plenty of room to move around.

Inside the run there should be fresh grass to nibble, but put some extra hay in and make sure there is plenty of fresh water. Cover one end of the run to provide shade and shelter, and don't forget that rabbits like to burrow, so the run should have a wire floor to stop your pet from digging its way out and running away.

Always keep an eye on your rabbit while it is in the run, in case there are cats or dogs around that might frighten it.

bits need to keep their teeth
l worn down, so that they can
properly.

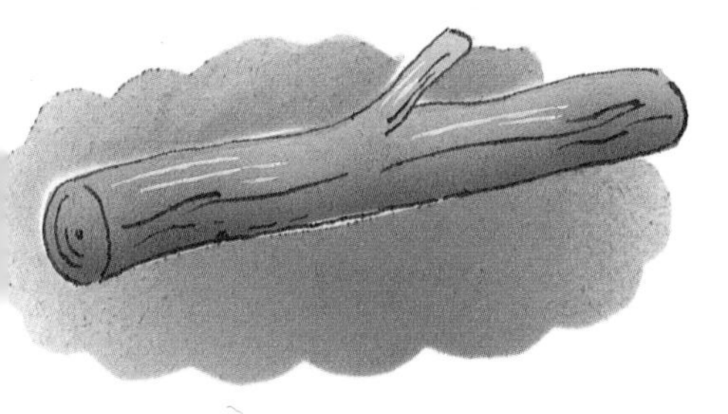

ten some small branches or
gs inside the hutch, so your
bit can gnaw on them. Fruit
wood is especially good.

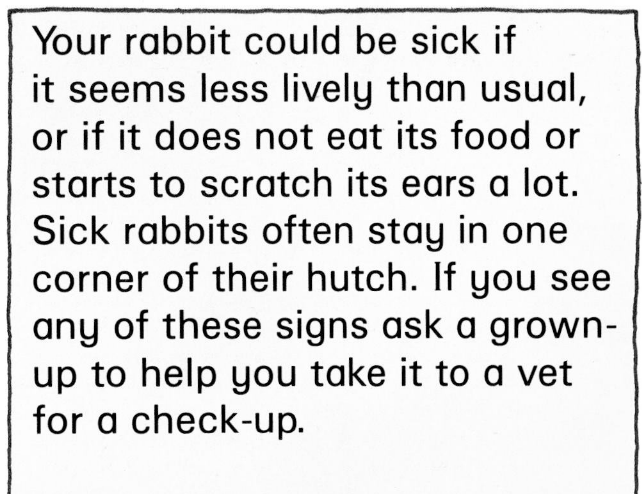

Your rabbit could be sick if it seems less lively than usual, or if it does not eat its food or starts to scratch its ears a lot. Sick rabbits often stay in one corner of their hutch. If you see any of these signs ask a grown-up to help you take it to a vet for a check-up.

A rabbit's claws can sometimes grow very long, and may need clipping. Teeth may also need to be clipped. If they grow too long your rabbit will not be able to eat. The vet will be able to do both these things for you.

Keeping Your Rabbit Clea

If you are careful to look after its hutch your rabbit will always be clean, healthy and happy, and there will be no smell or mess.

When you are cleaning, watch for holes or cracks which might let in cold or damp. If you see any you should ask someone to repair them for you.

You should clean the hutch out properly at least twice a week. It is a good idea to set aside regular days and times for cleaning — then y won't forget and your rabbit will get used to the routine.

hen you clean the hutch,
ange the straw or hay in the
eping box and put fresh
wdust or shavings on the floor.
member to clean the food
wls and drinking bottle as well.
Brush the floor of the hutch
d make sure you clean out
ery corner.

Have a safe place ready to put your rabbit while you do your cleaning. A cardboard box lined with newspaper will do. Keep any other pets away while your rabbit is out of its hutch.

Once a month ask a grown-up to help you give the hutch a really good clean with some soapy water and a brush. You can also buy a special cleaner to spray inside. Rinse the hutch well after you have cleaned it and make sure that everything has dried out before your rabbit goes back into its home.

Grooming

Rabbits are good at keeping themselves clean. They also enjoy being groomed, so you should brush your rabbit's coat now and then. Begin at the head and always brush gently in the direction that the fur grows.

A rabbit with a long-haired coat will need to be groomed at least once a week with a wide-toothed comb as well as a brush. This will stop the hai from tangling up into knots.

.t certain times of the year
ıbbits molt, which means that
ıey lose some of their old fur.
ou need to brush them more
ften at this time, to get rid of
ny loose hair.

Rabbits can become very tame and friendly if they are handled often and in the right way. When your rabbit has settled in you can begin to take it out of its hutch for a short time every day. It will soon get used to being held and will like to be petted. Give it lots of daily care and attention, but be patient when it is a new pet, and be careful not to frighten it.

.lways use both hands to
ently lift and hold your rabbit.
old it close to you, supporting
ıe back legs. Never try to pick
p a rabbit by its ears, because
ou could hurt it.

If your pet starts to kick, put
down right away, as it could
cratch you.

Do's and Don'ts

Here are some of the most important things to remember:

★**Do** give your rabbit lots of care and attention, but remember that if it does not want to be picked up, you should leave it alone.

★**Do** take your rabbit to the vet if it seems less lively than usual and you think it may be sick. Take it to the vet as soon as you can.

★**Do** clean out the hutch regularly – this will keep your rabbit healthy. Remember to throw away old food and always keep the bedding clean.

★**Do** give your rabbit something to gnaw at, such as a piece of wood. Our own teeth stop growing when we are adults, but rabbits' teeth keep on growing throughout their lives, ar gnawing will help to keep the worn down.

★**Do** keep two or three rabbi together if you like, but rememb that if you keep male and fema rabbits together you will soo have lots of baby rabbits to loo after.

★**Don't** let your rabbit out whe there are other animals aroun such as cats and dogs.

★**Don't** pick up your rabbit by i ears since this will hurt it. U both hands and support its hi legs when you lift it. Avo making quick movements whi may frighten it.

★**Don't** let your pet eat garde flowers, except for dandelion Some plants can make rabbi very sick.